# Is God Disappointed with Me?

Resting in God's Approval

Marc Davis

newgrowthpress.com

New Growth Press, Greensboro, NC 27401
newgrowthpress.com
Copyright © 2025 by Marc Davis

All rights reserved. No part of this publication may be reproduced, stored in a retrieval system, or transmitted in any form by any means, electronic, mechanical, photocopy, recording, or otherwise, without the prior permission of the publisher, except as provided by USA copyright law.

Unless otherwise indicated, Scripture quotations are taken from THE HOLY BIBLE, NEW INTERNATIONAL VERSION®, NIV® Copyright © 1973, 1978, 1984, 2011 by Biblica, Inc.® Used by permission. All rights reserved worldwide.

Scripture verses marked ESV are taken from The ESV® Bible (The Holy Bible, English Standard Version®). Copyright © 2001 by Crossway, a publishing ministry of Good News Publishers. The ESV® text has been reproduced in cooperation with and by permission of Good News Publishers. Unauthorized reproduction of this publication is prohibited. All rights reserved.

Cover Design: Dan Stelzer
Interior Typesetting and Ebook: Lisa Parnell, lparnellbookservices.com

ISBN: 978-1-64507-532-5 (print)
ISBN: 978-1-64507-533-2 (ebook)

Library of Congress Cataloging-in-Publication Data

Names: Davis, Marc B., author.
Title: Is God disappointed with me? : resting in God's approval / Marc Davis.
Description: Greensboro, NC : New Growth Press, [2025]
Identifiers: LCCN 2025000355 (print) | LCCN 2025000356 (ebook) | ISBN 9781645075325 | ISBN 9781645075332 (ebook)
Subjects: LCSH: Self-confidence—Religious aspects—Christianity. | Change (Psychology)—Religious aspects—Christianity.
Classification: LCC BV4598.23 .D38 2025 (print) | LCC BV4598.23 (ebook) | DDC 248.4—dc23/eng/20250216
LC record available at https://lccn.loc.gov/2025000355
LC ebook record available at https://lccn.loc.gov/2025000356

Printed in India

29 28 27 26 25     1 2 3 4 5

Think about this for a moment: If God were to turn his gaze specifically to you and let his eyes linger there, what would his facial expression be? What body language would accompany the words he might say to you?

Many Christians have a hard time imagining that God would look at them with a warm smile of affection and delight. For many, their immediate reaction is to imagine God regarding them with an eye roll, a face palm, a sigh, a frown, or folded arms of frustration. Why?

This gut reaction is born out of a deep sense that we don't measure up. God knows our failures, large and small, in intimate detail—not just our long-ago failures, but our present-day shortcomings too. Sometimes it seems like examples crowd one on top of another in our minds; we can't consider one before the next one interrupts and adds its accusation on top of the last.

The variety of failures is something to behold. You yelled at the kids. You left the car window open and the interior got soaked in the rain. You had good intentions to have the new neighbors over for a barbecue, but somehow the summer came and went and it never happened. You spent the better part of an evening rehashing an old resentment. You got a gym membership but haven't been there for three months. A hundred things. Surely God is looking at you and shaking his head, wishing you would just get your act together. Right?

## Understanding Our Inner Dialogue

Each of us has an inward life of thoughts and impressions, an inner dialogue that runs in the background of our busy and chaotic lives. We may not even be fully aware of many of the ideas that pass through our heads as we drive to work, wash the dishes, or mow the lawn. Some of our thoughts are coherent and well-developed, while others are only vague and half-cooked. But even a vague, unarticulated idea can be very powerful, a whispered word in our ears that robs us of joy and courage.

The persistent thought *God is disappointed with me* resonates with more people than you might think. It quietly finds space in the hearts and minds of even longtime followers of Jesus, people who trust Christ for salvation but who nonetheless are troubled by a lingering notion that God somehow disapproves of them.

Here is our task together: We're going to engage this idea of God's attitude toward us. We're going to hold our thoughts up to the light—to what God actually says in the Bible—and invite him to help us sort them out.

## Is God Disappointed Because I'm Weak?

There are two ways in which our sense of our own poor performance might cause us to feel that God must surely be frustrated or disappointed with us. The first has to do with failures that expose us as weak or incompetent. The following examples might feel familiar:

- I forgot to do something important at work, and I let people down.
- I tried to make a nice home-cooked meal for a loved one's birthday, but it turned out badly.
- I failed to meet a vocational goal that was important to me. I always wanted to be a doctor, and my whole extended family knew that and celebrated it—but then I couldn't get through organic chemistry.
- I overslept again and didn't spend time with the Lord.
- I had five things on my to-do list today, and I sort of did one of them, but not very well.
- I tried to do a home repair, but I ended up making things worse and we had to pay someone to fix my mess.
- I got tongue-tied and completely missed the opportunity to share Christ when my neighbor asked me about my faith.
- I was in a car accident and it was my fault.

Sometimes even minor, silly things seem to weigh a lot. It was my daughter's school picture day, and I completely forgot and sent her in with her hair uncombed, wearing her brother's old sweatshirt.

Maybe you can relate to some of these failures—and add more to the list.

Do any of these examples involve sin issues? Maybe, on some level. Maybe my driving mistake stemmed from a failure to love my neighbor by paying adequate attention to my surroundings. But for the most part, these failures are expressions of weakness rather than sin. I just didn't measure up. It's not so much that I feel guilty when these things happen—it's that I feel like an idiot. We hate being incompetent, letting people down, or even letting ourselves down.

When confronted with the reality of our various failures, the negative narrative in our heads can turn into a deafening roar. The message from the universe—and maybe from God—seems to be *what's the matter with you?*

A slightly different but related question can torment us: *What do you have to show for yourself?* This question tends to surface on milestone birthdays, or at high school reunions, or whenever you find yourself in the company of people you see only occasionally. The sting of the question comes from comparison—measuring yourself against other people who took a different life path, pursued a different education, or have a different family makeup. Perhaps they have a nicer house, are more well-known, or are living out a dream you once aspired to. You find yourself observing other people's lives and feeling condemned as you think about your own life.

That condemnation can express itself in second-guessing life decisions even many years after the fact. It's as if every decision you ever made, even prayerful, well-considered decisions, suddenly all come under question. You might think, *Why didn't I get my MBA? Why did I stay near home instead of moving to California when I had the chance?* Never mind that you had good reasons for your choices.

Relational or family disappointment can also carry heavy emotional freight. Disappointment stemming from an absence of close friendships, the lack of a spouse, or a failed relationship—maybe a divorce—can take you beyond the sadness of loneliness to feel more like a painful verdict on your own person. You feel like *you* are a disappointment, like something is fundamentally wrong with you. Relational struggle can become part of the larger chorus of negative messages that you internalize about yourself.

Any of these struggles alone could be challenged by a kind, reasonable friend who would remind you, "You're not thinking about this the right way. That's just not true!" But the difficulty is that a stubborn objectivity surrounds many of these experiences. I know that I missed the mark—I'm not imagining it. I know that other people have succeeded in areas where I have failed.

Some of your failures have impacted other people. Sometimes others communicate—implicitly or explicitly—that they are disappointed in you. Messages from important people in your life play on a loop in your head. The cumulative effect is something like an ultimate, cosmic Yelp review: "Two stars. Disappointing."

## Is God Disappointed Because I'm a Sinner?

But it's not just a matter of natural human frailty. We're also sinners. We go our own way, think only of ourselves, indulge wrong desires, or disregard the ways we are called to love others. And this isn't just ancient history! Some of these sin patterns may be deeply ingrained into our lives in the present. Perhaps one or more of the following scenarios sound familiar:

- You lose your temper.
- You indulge a sexual fantasy—maybe you use pornography or daydream about someone you know.
- You speak poorly of someone, tearing them down to someone else.
- You waste time on your phone when you're on the clock or when you have important work to do.

- You complain about your own home/car/spouse and envy someone else's.
- You rehearse someone else's bad behavior in your mind and wallow in resentment.
- You eat too much, drink too much, sleep too much, work too much, or spend too much.

And it wasn't the first time! You've felt bad—you've said you wouldn't do it again. You were genuinely sad about what you did. And now you've done it again. Lather, rinse, repeat.

The repetition is much of what's so crushing. It's not just a matter of feeling guilty; it's also an embarrassment, a source of deep shame. Again, you feel like a failure, a hot mess. *What's the matter with me?*

Perhaps your theology seems to condemn you too. You know that believers in Jesus are forgiven for their sins—but thereafter their lives are supposed to be different. Jesus does more than just cleanse us of our sin; he delivers us from its power. This is what you've believed. Maybe this is what you've taught others. But your life does not seem to bear it out. *Why didn't it work?* Embarrassed, you're afraid to share your struggle with others. You think, *Am I even a real Christian? If I am a real Christian, I'm a grade-D Christian, an underachiever.*

There seems to be little of the Lord's power on display in your life. *Surely God is disappointed with me*, you think; *I'm certainly disappointed with myself!*

## Receiving Grace as the Weak and Wayward

As you can see, there are large questions at stake here concerning what you believe about yourself and about God. Which narrative has the right to serve as the controlling paradigm for how you understand yourself and your place in the world—for how you understand God's heart toward you? Are you the sum of your actions or your failures to act? Are you defined by your weakness and your sins? Or does God have a better word for you—a word of grace?

If you have laid hold of Jesus, let me suggest that the deepest, truest idea about you is this: *You are not under the law, but under grace* (Romans 6:14). When you are "under the law," your performance is what defines your identity and security, your place in the universe, and your relationship with God. These are the controlling questions every day: How did I do? Did I keep the rules? Did I hit the mark? Did I accomplish the goal?

But if you are "under grace," everything is fundamentally different. Your identity, security, and status with God are not up for grabs. They do not fluctuate based on your performance. Your whole self, from first to last, in its entirety, every day from now through eternity, has been established on an infinitely more secure foundation.

On what basis do you live and breathe and relate to God, to people, and to the world? Only on this basis: *God has initiated a relationship with you in Christ based on his love for you—and nothing else.* He has extended his kindness to you in Jesus. What he has initiated, he will follow through on; he will not change his mind. You are under grace forever.

This is truth, etched in stone. God has declared it over you. But it's also a living, moving, new idea because as you take hold of grace as the controlling principle of your life, it will be worked out in a thousand directions, applied to every corner of who you are and how you function.

Jesus compared the kingdom of God to "yeast that a woman took and mixed into about sixty pounds of flour until it worked all through the dough" (Matthew 13:33). Similarly, the principles of the kingdom (and grace is the first principle of the kingdom) have far-reaching application, with transformative implications. The truth of being "under grace" will change your self-conception from A to Z. Where the law beats you down with accusation and condemnation, grace allows you to stand up straight and look people in the eye. As you understand that God's gaze on you is kind and compassionate, God the Father, the "lifter of my head" (Psalm 3:3 ESV), will enable you to increasingly return his gaze. His love for you strengthens you from the inside out; it builds you up so that you begin to function in the world as a restored human being with dignity and worth. Your love for him begins to flower in response to his love for you, and it works itself out in love for your neighbor.

## Help for Weak People

How does the principle of grace apply when we feel weak and incompetent? What does it have to do with the unfinished to-do list or the botched home repair?

As we noted above, sometimes our deficiencies are colored in part by negligence, or carelessness, or a lack of love—in short, a sin issue. What do we do then? We'll speak to this more below, but the short answer is *repent and believe.* Take it to Jesus. Tell him what you did or failed to do. Receive his grace, ask for his strength, and move on.

It's different when we struggle with the burden of our own incompetence. In this case, your prayer might be, "Oh Lord, I want to be good at things! I don't want to make so many mistakes. I want to be efficient, productive, and successful, and I'm so very frustrated that often I'm not." But as you pray about these things, you may find that the principle of grace speaks to your frustration by undercutting the importance of performance. We feel our mistakes so acutely because we believe so deeply that our performance determines our identity, security, and status. But guess what? It doesn't.

Sometimes we operate under an assumption that we *should* be good at things. Why? Because other people are good at those things. But that assumption is flawed. God has not made all his creatures the same. A tiger can't fly. A dolphin can't come out of the water to climb a tree. As a human being, you're made in the image of God. It's an amazing thing to be a man or a woman. And yet, at the same time, weakness is baked into you.

I want to suggest that weakness is not only part of fallen humanity; it's part of *un*fallen humanity. God made you to be dependent—in need of help, ultimately from him but also from others around you. And this is good.

Each of us has our areas of relative competency, our God-given aptitudes and abilities, and also our areas of incompetency. We're good at some things and not at others. We make mistakes, and we get things wrong. That's all self-evident. The question is, can I be comfortable in my own skin as a mere mortal? Can I rest in the love of God for me that does not depend on my being a straight-A student, *and* captain of the team, *and* the lead in the school play? Can it be very much okay for me to live a quieter, more understated life in an average community, working a job that fits my skill sets, loving the particular family God has given me, serving my local church, and seeking to live a life of faithfulness to God?

The Lord is inviting you to get comfortable in your skin as a weak human being. We chafe against that; we don't like it at all. But the Lord says, don't chafe. You may want to consider whether your desire to be strong and competent is linked to a proud desire to be independent, not needing anyone's help. If so, take it to Jesus, confess what you see in your heart, and ask for his help.

I'm not telling you to be unambitious. Sometimes it's good to aspire to learn to do something that does not come naturally. You can work hard, learn, and get better at things. You can set a challenging goal and apply yourself diligently to achieving it, and sometimes, with God's help, you will succeed. But the reality is that we will never be good at everything—and that's absolutely okay. Our performance is not the sum total of our life.

What about the question, what do you have to show for yourself? Once more, there are different strands to sort out in our complex histories. For instance, I may have been a lazy student who didn't make the most of my educational opportunities, and now I regret that deeply and wish I could go back to have another chance at it. Again, I have something to take to Christ—he welcomes me as one under grace to come to him for forgiveness of past sins, along with fresh wisdom and help for the present. What's done is done; his grace covers it and allows me to look to the future with hope.

But my lack of success, wealth, or reputation is probably not a result of sin—in fact, it's not even something to be worried about. Sometimes we need the Lord to say to us again, "Stop comparing yourself to other people. Keep your eyes on me." As Jesus said to Peter when Peter compared John's future life to his own, "What is that to you? You must follow me" (John 21:22).

The Lord was sovereign over your past, he is with you in the present, and he calls you not to prominence, but to a life of love (Ephesians 5:2). The idea of "being somebody" may die hard, but the reality is that some things are better than prominence. Again, if you've made an idol of wealth or success or some vision of the good life that you haven't attained, repent and believe. Take it to Jesus. Tell him about it. Ask him to reorient you so that you value what he values.

## Help for Sinners

Repentance is both possible and normal when we live under grace. When I learn to live as a well-loved child of God, unafraid because I'm under grace, coming to Jesus with my sin becomes a regular part of life, as everyday as eating and sleeping. Sin is never to be taken lightly, but it's also not surprising, and it does not torpedo who I am or my security in that identity. People who need grace have a path to follow, and it always leads back to Jesus. Then, like the Father in the story of the two sons, God's heart and the heart of Christ are always welcoming toward repentant sinners (Luke 15)! He does not shame us when we come to him; he embraces us.

But sometimes a pattern of sin becomes entrenched and seemingly impossible to break, and leads to a deep sense of failure and shame before God. In this case, we must all the more cling to the grace that is ours in Christ. Consider the words of pastor Jack Miller:

> The heart of growing as a Christian and helping others to grow is discovering that the fight with our sin is not just hard and difficult, but impossible. We can't solve the simplest problem without grace. If you go into battle without Jesus, you will fail. When we come to the impossible and are broken again and again, that's when we cry out to Jesus for grace. That's what changes yourself and others. That's the heart of growing to be like Christ.[1]

This may come as news to you: Many, if not all, believers in Jesus struggle in some way with some pattern of behavior that just seems to "have their number." You're not the only one. In his love and wisdom, God often uses this kind of struggle to take us deeper in our relationship with him.

Meditate on this and internalize it: The heart of sin—all kinds of sin—is willful independence. We want to do life on our own terms, to be in charge, to stand on our own two feet. We don't want to be a burden on anyone. The chorus we often repeat is, "I've got it. I'm good." But then some struggle just brings us to our knees, and we are totally unable to handle it with our own resources. God often uses exactly this sort of thing to break us more deeply of our intractable desire for independence. We begin to realize (as Jack Miller told us more than once), *I'm worse than I think. I don't just need a little help; I need a big Savior whose grace is enough for big sinners.*

You will likely require help to break the pattern that enslaves you. Often God's help comes to us through a wise brother or sister. To climb a repentance mountain of this magnitude, you will need the support of someone who has some history and wisdom with the "deep waters" of the sinful human heart (Proverbs 20:5). It will be embarrassing to share your struggle with another person, but this too is part of the cure—God will use this step to begin to kill your pride. As you seek that person out, ponder these points:

- You cannot cherish the root sin and expect the visible sin to magically disappear. Sin is not just a matter of visible external behaviors, but of deep subterranean patterns of thought and attitude and corrupt desire. We cannot just pick dandelion heads and expect that our dandelion problem is solved; we will need to go deep to address the root problem, the sin under the sin. You will need to give Jesus access there.

- You will need to nurture a posture of dependence toward God that is much more far-reaching and pervasive than you have before. For instance, if you have a problem with pornography use, I expect it often occurs late in the evening. You cannot function independently all day and then expect that at 10 p.m. your love of independence will not be firmly in the driver's seat. You will need to learn the truth of the old hymn "I Need Thee Every Hour" and adopt a new heart posture of needy dependence that characterizes the day from morning until night. Ask Jesus to show you how to live in this way.

Let this be your great encouragement: Jesus is "a friend of . . . sinners" (Luke 7:34). His heart of compassion goes out to the one who is defeated by sin. He is in it with you for the long haul, and what he began he will finish (Philippians 1:6). The work that you are doing now to grow in dependence on Jesus and to kill sin is not done as someone under the law, but as a man or a woman under grace. His love for you overarches this struggle; it plays out under an umbrella of secure, unfluctuating kindness. He is for you in it.

## Living Under Grace, Walking in Obedience

Some will still think, *Surely, though, when I sin, God is disappointed with me, isn't he?* Let me answer in this way.

Ponder again (and again and again) what it means to be under grace. Above I referred to the image of being under an umbrella. Do you imagine an umbrella that is flimsy, that blows in the wind and still leaves you wet in a rainstorm? Instead, think of grace like an enormous dome that reaches up to the sky and extends for miles in every direction. You will live your whole life under the dome of God's grace. You cannot wander out from under it. If you are attached to Jesus, the Father says the same about you as he did about Jesus at the time of his baptism: "This is my son [daughter] whom I love; with him [her] I am well pleased" (Matthew 3:17). That is set in stone. The whole of your existence from here on out happens under the dome of God's grace.

But there is a repeated theme in Scripture that is also worth thinking about. In numerous places in the New Testament epistles, we find language of living to please God. Consider the following partial list of examples:

- "Find out what pleases the Lord" (Ephesians 5:10).
- "We make it our goal to please him" (2 Corinthians 5:9).
- "We instructed you how to live in order to please God, as in fact you are living. Now we ask and urge you in the Lord Jesus to do this more and more" (1 Thessalonians 4:1).
- "Do not forget to do good and to share with others, for with such sacrifices God is pleased" (Hebrews 13:16).

We don't do justice to this teaching of God's approval in Christ if we say, "Remember that you are under grace! It doesn't matter anymore if you sin." In fact, in Romans 6:14 Paul makes the appeal, "You are not under the law, but under grace" to argue the exact opposite: it is exactly *because* we are under grace that we must be careful not to allow sin to be our master. Similarly, the same logic applies in all of these verses: because you are under grace, make it your goal to please God.

What's the opposite of pleasing the Lord? It seems clear that it is displeasing him. And it's not unbiblical or anti-gospel to say that a Christian's actions can be displeasing to God. Consider the story of David and Bathsheba in 2 Samuel 11. At the end of the chapter, the author summarizes it neatly: "But the thing David had done displeased the LORD" (2 Samuel 11:27). Of course David's sin displeased God—it was wicked! And sometimes the things we do displease God too.

But it is important to emphasize that while our human idea of God's disappointment is often full of exasperation and low on hope, this biblical idea of God's displeasure carries none of those implications. God's displeasure does not cause him to withdraw from you. It causes him to move toward you! His heart for sinners is one of compassion. He pursues you with kindness, inviting you to repentance because he longs to be gracious to you and restore you to health and wholeness. He has not given up on you; he is setting before you a hopeful vision of better things, and he delights to see you grow into it.

What do we do when we're aware that we've displeased the Lord? Here we circle back to what we said earlier: repent and believe. You and I need grace, not just in a once-and-done manner, but in an ongoing manner. James 4:6 offers these lovely, hopeful words: "But he gives us more grace." This happens every day as we bring our failures to Jesus.

## Living with Hope

Let me leave you with this encouragement: As we live under the dome of grace, growing in love for the One who loved us first, growing in a desire to do what is right and live a life of love, the Lord meets us! He surrounds our efforts to please him with more grace. He is delighted by our fumbling, imperfect fits and starts of obedience. We are growing into our identity as God's children, beginning in small ways to "live as Jesus did" (1 John 2:6). Because we know we're under grace, because we're cast in dependence on Jesus for everything, our lives are beginning to show glimmers of Christ to the world. This is true of you too. And your Father is so pleased with what he sees.

Let me spell it out: God's heart of grace toward you is much bigger than any displeasure he has with your remaining sin. He may call you to repentance and obedience—take that seriously and do not neglect it. But know that admonition flows from his kind heart. *He is not disappointed with you.* If you are in Christ, grace frames your identity and frames God's heart toward you. The more you treasure this idea and let it get hold of your heart, the more your life will blossom with the freedom of life in him.

Perhaps a short summary will be helpful as you continue to process these themes in the days ahead. When you feel like God must be disappointed with you, what can you do?

1. *Preach the gospel to yourself.* Remember that you are entirely approved in Christ, by grace through faith. This approval has nothing to do with your performance.

2. *Let yourself be human.* Understand that your limitations and need to depend on God and others are part of how God made you.
3. *Learn the rhythms of daily repentance, and grow in your understanding of God's character.* He is a welcoming Father who always receives repentant sinners kindly.
4. *Aspire to live as Jesus did and do what pleases him because he loves you.* Depend on him hour by hour to help you in this.
5. *Be hopeful because of the gospel!* Give yourself grace and continuously receive more grace from the Father.

May the Lord encourage you deeply with the message of the gospel of grace, delivered by his Spirit to the deepest places of your heart.

## Endnote

1. Jack Miller, *Saving Grace: Daily Devotions from Jack Miller* (New Growth Press, 2014), 305.

# resources
## for Continued Spiritual Growth

*Every day around the world, Serge teams help people develop and deepen a living, breathing, growing relationship with Jesus. We help people connect with God in ways that are genuinely grace-motivated and increase desire and ability to reach out to others. Whether you are a church leader, actively engaged in ministry, or just seeking to go deeper in your relationship with God – we have resources that can help.*

### Grace-Centered Teaching Events

Both scripture and our own experience tell us that this side of heaven we will never outgrow our need for God's renewing grace. Serge was founded on the principle that missionaries and ministers of the gospel - whether vocational or not - need to hear and experience ongoing reminders of the gospel just as much as the ones they are trying to reach. Serge hosts periodic conferences as one way we seek to nurture this continual dynamic of grace leading to mission, including in North America. While the content and format of the weekends can vary, these events consistently feature transformative biblical teaching, authentic stories of how the gospel changes us, and small group interaction – all aimed at cultivating personal gospel renewal that frees you and propels you into missional living.

### Webinars and Podcasts

Serge's webinars and podcasts are free and easy ways to regularly hear grace-centered teaching from a variety of presenters - both Serge and non-Serge. With a broad range of topics like parenting, personal growth, leadership, and ministry, these conversations will help you apply the gospel to more and more areas of your everyday life and relationships.

### Books and Studies

Serge has a growing collection of grace-centered publications that bring together grace-based theology with materials and teaching to help you live out the gospel in every part of your life. Whether you are looking for personal devotionals, small group studies, guidance for ministry, or honest and compelling stories from the mission field, our books and studies can encourage your faith and help you grow in your understanding and experience of God's grace.

---

Serge — Grace at the Fray

**Visit us online at:**
serge.org/books-and-studies

newgrowthpress.com